TRIPOLI

PORTRAIT OF A CITY

for Vincent de Luca
with best wishes

Philip Ward

Other books on Libya
by the same author

Seldom Rains: Libyan Poems   (*Oleander Press*, 1967)
Touring Libya: the Western Provinces   (*Faber and Faber*, 1967)
Apuleius on Trial at Sabratha   (*Oleander Press*, 1968)
Touring Libya: the Southern Provinces   (*Faber and Faber*, 1968)
At the Best of Times: Libyan Poems   (*Oleander Press*, 1968)
Touring Libya: the Eastern Provinces   (*Faber and Faber*, 1969)

Tripoli's Suq al-Mushir, where Old and New
Tripoli meet, with the mid-nineteenth century
Clock Tower (Turkish period) in the
background.

TRIPOLI
PORTRAIT OF A CITY

BY

PHILIP WARD

THE OLEANDER PRESS

Copyright by Philip Ward 1969

Designed by Derek Maggs

Printed by
Ditchling Press, Ditchling, Hassocks, Sussex

Contents

Illustrations and Maps

Front cover: A Tripolitanian pilgrim carrying the Libyan flag.

Frontispiece: Tripoli's Suq al-Mushir, where Old and New Tripoli meet, with the mid-nineteenth-century Clock Tower (Turkish period) in the background.

Preface

My principal concern while writing *Touring Libya: the Western Provinces* (1967) was to display the lesser-known attractions of western Libya at the expense of the region's greatest treasure: the city of Tripoli.

Now the time of reckoning has come, and in this book I portray her (for she is feminine) in some of her many moods, omitting only what was described at any length in my earlier book.

This guide is the first in English to be devoted solely to Tripoli, and though it may be foolhardy to venture into print at a time of energetic renewal like the present, my consolation is that enough of old Tripoli will always survive to bestow piquancy on the dullest text. The skyline changes every year but the atmosphere remains.

How best to characterise this atmosphere? Indefinable in a few words, I hope it will take form in the reader's imagination when he puts down this portrait of a city geographically near Malta and Italy, spiritually akin to Wahhabi Saudi Arabia, and economically allied to the other lands of the Maghrib: Tunisia, Algeria, and Morocco.

It is as pleasant to thank all my Tripolitan friends for their conversation and discussion while I was preparing this book as it is impossible to list all their names. However I must acknowledge specific help from Cav. Mario Fabbri, Salim A. Arayed, P. Giacinto Ravasi, and W. D. Peyton. Angelo Pesce kindly took many photographs for this book, and Tihamer Kover supplied the coloured frontispiece to symbolise the meeting, on equal terms, of the Old Tripoli with the New.

PHILIP WARD
Tripoli
July 1969

I

The Edge of the Desert

Tripoli is a city of a quarter of a million people surrounded on the north by the Mediterranean Sea and on the south by the Jafara – or alluvial plain – from which rise the encircling Western Mountains, giving way in turn to the arid Hammada al-Hamra' (or Red Plateau) and the desert.

Visitors arriving from Europe by aeroplane fly over the coast near Tripoli and, after another thirty kilometres' descent, land at Tripoli Airport, set in the fertile coastal belt amid olive plantations. The drive from the airport to Tripoli begins along eucalyptus avenues, and continues past the characteristic village of Qasr bin Ghashir through unspoilt country with palms, bushes, small-holdings, square white houses on the horizon (the few by the roadside are mainly shops), and above all sand – not the high dunes of the hinterland, but a soft, snow-like sheet that covers everything but the houses, vegetation, and the road ahead.

For no matter how many buildings go up along the airport road in years to come, sand will always reveal that Tripoli is on the edge of the desert. While walking down its broad Independence Avenue (in Arabic Jaddat Istiqlal), its palm-lined Shar'a Adrian Pelt (street named after the United Nations Commissioner who did more than any other foreigner to ensure Libya's easy passage to independence in 1951), or its busy, commercial Jaddat 'Umar al-Mukhtar (an avenue named for the great Libyan martyr and patriot), one is tempted to consider Tripoli not only a cosmopolitan city of great charm – which it is – but also as the centre of Libya, the nucleus from which all routes diverge.

This may well be commercially true in the twentieth century when Libyan Arab Republic airline routes connect her with Rome, Paris,

Geneva, London, Athens, Cairo, Beirut, and other capitals, but historically Tripoli is simply a terminus or a starting point. The 'centres' for commerce even up to the end of the nineteenth century were Ghadames, Murzuq, and Ghat. These oases were the focal points from which caravan-routes radiated to all points of the compass – where fortunes were made and lost, according to market fluctuations and the stamina of camels and men.

It is important to realise that the Libyan Arab Republic is a union of exceedingly complex and varied ethnic components: Tubbu in the Tibesti plains, Tuareg nomads in the south-west, Beduin in the great eastern expanses of *sarir*, town Arab in Benghazi and Tripoli. A nation has been welded from elements so disparate that the parallel of the United States or the Soviet Union must be sought: but in the case of Libya the unity is much more real than apparent – it is not an accidental union conceived by politicians, but a true nation whose language is Arabic, and whose religion is Islam.

Tripoli is only a tiny corner of this nation and the pity of it is that so many foreign residents and tourists in Libya never venture outside Tripoli to explore the glories of Libya's past and the outstanding achievements since independence.

There is, perhaps, no help for it: tourism being considered as a status symbol rather than a mode of self-exploration, it is perhaps only necessary to have visited Tripoli, and then go on via Benghazi to Cairo, or via Tunis to Algiers. But he who has not seen more of Libya than Tripoli has not seen Tripoli. In fact, my deepest revelation of Tripoli's character came from seeing Sebha: here in the desert a town rising from the sand with the faith and industry that would have been apparent in the building of Tripoli's old city when, in 643, the Arab forces of Amr ibn al-As took the decaying Byzantine harbour-town and ensured that for centuries to come Tripoli and Libya would be Muslim.

Again, the piety of Libyan Muslims can only be understood against the background of the Sanusi movement that at its height swept across the Islamic World from Morocco to Persia, establishing a *zawia* (a religious institution embodying a rest-room for travellers, a Quranic school, and a residence for religious teachers) in dozens of cities and hundreds of lesser towns.

Kufra, Jaghbub and Zawiat al-Baida – all in the Eastern Provinces – have at one time or another all been the headquarters of the Sanusi, and the humility and asceticism of this great movement are evident in Tripoli if the curious traveller will open his eyes, heart and mind to the pulse of the city.

Waha, Raguba, Dahra, Zelten, Nafura, Hofra, Augila, Sarir: all these alien names denote vast oil-fields whose outlets on the Syrtic Coast (at Ras as-Sidra, Marsa Brega, Ras al-Unuf, Zuwaitina, and Tobruk are counted among the busiest oil-terminals on the African continent. The traveller who comes to Tripoli now will sense prosperity: but he will see no rigs or pipelines. Oil company offices provide the only outward evidence that Tripoli is the backroom city for an industry which accounts for over 98 % of the value of Libya's exports.

A great sports city (built for the Pan-Arab Games of 1974) rises in the suburb of Gurgi. A whole new suburb of luxury villas has grown up at Giorgimpopoli, west of Tripoli. A vivid contrast to Giorgimpopoli is provided by the fertile area just to the east of Tripoli named after its Friday Market, Suq al-Jum'a, or by the Agricultural Experimental Station at Sidi al-Misri, with its miniature zoo and its tranquil Cypress Lake, on the road to Leptis Magna.

In the centre of this diversity and itself a microcosm of great variety, is Tripoli's Old City, with its noisy, colourful medley of shopkeepers, bright-eyed urchins, modestly-veiled Libyan women, Maltese and Italians bumped into at unlikely corners, cyclists whistling, more shopkeepers, donkeys with carts demonstrably wider than the alley, wise old men with kindly eyes, and yet more shopkeepers.

I defy any writer to describe Tripoli in all its moods. This short book aims to do no more than convey a genuine flavour of some aspects of Trabulus al-Gharb (Tripoli of the West) to readers who wish they were here, or wish they were still here. Or to a third category of readers: those who are glad they are still here.

2
Tripoli in May

I sit, eyes half-closed, at a garden café, and look out on a broad Mediterranean harbour: a harbour found by the Phoenicians, fortified by the Romans, and established by later rulers: the harbour of Tripoli. Moored rowing-boats drift near the jetty; a fast Mercedes passes a horse-drawn cab – the *'arabiya* or gharry. A wary cat rubs his head against my ankle, its eyes appealing. The sky is a perfect, unclouded blue. A street vendor pauses in front of me with pens, combs and watches, hoping to haggle and sell, but neither persists, nor looks disappointed when I shrug my shoulders.

I have walked from Shar'a Mizran along Shar'a Haiti, across Maidan al-Jaza'ir (which is Cathedral Square), past the long, low Parliament Building, and so to my favourite harbour café. I relax in the spring breeze with a soft drink, and watch passers-by strolling leisurely in groups of two or three down the wide avenues, shady with porticoes, towards the massive Seraglio. The shouting of Naples port has softened to conversation: the gesticulations of Marseilles have modulated from fierce to gentle. The excitability of northern Mediterranean shores has become a passive harmony of shy friendliness and quiet. One holidays in Tripoli to laze.

A carpet-seller on a bicycle passes, pointing to his load with eyebrows raised in encouraging enquiry. A muezzin calls to prayer from a mosque nearby and the lapping sea absorbs the echo.

An atmosphere of brightness has something to do with Tripoli's year-round loveliness: shimmering whiteness all but dazzles the surprised eye. The darkness has a gleaming, pulsing quality that those who do not know Africa cannot imagine. Sand polishes clean. Most new buildings that challenge the Tripoli skyline are a bold white. The warm brown of the Castle and the rose-tinged cathedral (whose spire is the sailor's first glimpse of Africa) subtly vary the colour of Tripoli.

Northern eyes are accustomed to penetrating through fog, or at the least an industrial haze. Tripoli light acts as a contact lens; there is no filter for the actuality of things, which are seen in all their utter truthfulness. I wear sun-glasses even in winter to avoid the shock of light so acute.

Tripoli is a place to be lived in: it can only be appreciated to the full after long and detailed explorations. The visitor who walks quickly, purposefully, down Shar'a 24 December completely misses the piquant contrasts between the shady Islamic School of Arts and Crafts, of the Turkish period, tiny Italian shops selling groceries and fruit, a Libyan bookshop, an Indian merchant, and vast American oil company offices. Nothing clashes: it appears rather that an imaginative internationalism has found a home to proclaim itself.

3
Wind and Weather

Strong the Giblee *wind is blowing*
JOHN GREENLEAF WHITTIER

Tripoli enjoys an ideal Mediterranean climate, with a daily average high of 61°F in Winter and 86°F in Summer. There is virtually no rainfall between June and September, when beaches are full and office-workers wear short-sleeved shirts or light summer dresses. Some rain falls every winter, but snow last fell in the Western Mountains south of Tripoli as long ago as February 1952. Fog is never experienced, but early morning sea mist is common.

The only weather-worry in Tripoli is an occasional *qibli*, or hot sand-storm. The *Qibla* (an Arabic word for the direction of Mecca) is the barren south – the Hammada al-Hamra' and its surrounding desert country. A hot wind rises from the Sahara, increasing in speed and dryness as it crosses the hot, flat plateau-country.

Herodotus related how the fearsome *qibli* destroyed the Libyan tribe of Psylli by drying up all their water, leaving them to die of thirst.

James Bruce, in his *Travels to discover the source of the Nile*, called it 'the simoom' (probably from the Arabic *samma*, to poison) writing that it 'still continued to blow, so as to exhaust us entirely'. In his *Manfred*, Byron conjured up 'the red-hot breath of the most lone simoom which dwells but in the desert'.

Keysler, the eighteenth-century traveller, tells how 'the woods south of Rome are kept up as a fence against the *sirocco*, or south-west wind', sirocco being an Italian corruption of *sharq*, the Arabic for 'east'.

The Tripoli *qibli* can blow up at any time of year, but is most usual at a sudden change of season, between May and June or in early

Autumn. The wind invariably settles down within three days, but while it lasts Mediterranean clarity is offended: the sea turns grey, and the sky clouds over a dusty brown.

A *qibli* can be predicted when a sudden drop in barometric pressure coincides with low humidity. The weather may be calm, but if the morning air is dry, the sun pale, and the sky grey with high, reddish golden clouds, a *qibli* may swirl up by the middle of the afternoon.

4
Early Tripoli

The earliest surviving form of name for a settlement at Tripoli is the neo-Punic *Wy't*, pronounced either *Uiat* or *Wayat*. In Roman times this became *Oea*, and when Diocletian became Emperor in 284 A.D., the *provincia Tripolitana* (or 'province of the three cities') was formed in eastern Africa Proconsularis. The three cities in question were then known as Sabrat(h)a, Oea, and Leptis, and at that time the *praeses* ('governor' in Latin) probably resided at Leptis, the most populous and affluent city of the province.

But with the gradual decline of her sister-cities, Oea took over the leadership of the coast and began to assume the name *Tripolis*, meaning 'three cities'. Though dropped in Italian, the last letter is retained in the modern Arabic form *Trabulus*, in which the non-Arabic letters 'p' and 'o' change to 'b' and neutral 'u'. Officially, the adjective 'western' is suffixed to Trabulus, giving *Trabulus al-Gharb*, to distinguish it from its eastern namesake *Trabulus ash-Sham* (Syrian Tripoli), which today is in Lebanon.

So far, so good. Nobody will disagree with this summary. Where the controversy arises is in the interpretation of Tripoli's previous names.

Boni and Mariani have claimed that the site of Oea was occupied in prehistoric times, but the first permanent settlers on the Libyan coast may have been the Phoenicians, who are thought to have arrived in Tripolitania between the twelfth and tenth centuries B.C. Cádiz in Spain and Utique in Tunisia are believed to have been colonised by the Phoenicians about 1100 B.C., and the establishment of a post at Oea may well have been roughly contemporary with these foundations.

Mueller believes that the name *Oea* comes ultimately from the

Libyan (pre-Arabic) word *Ait*, from which the form found on neo-Punic coins – *Uiat* – is derived. The original name may thus have been a compound including *Ait*, or 'tribe', and the name of the tribe, subsequently lost. This hypothesis is supported by the modern practice of naming rural districts after the name of the principal tribe inhabiting each one, such as the Qabila Taridia ('Taridia tribe') of the Mudiriat ar-Rujban, near Jadu.

The 'Stadiasmus Maris Magni' calls the town *Makaria*, which refers to Melqart, a Punic god identified by the Greeks with Hercules. A coin – so much information that has otherwise disappeared can be found on coins – has the interesting inscription *Oeath bilath Ma'kar*, meaning 'Oea, town of Melqart' (cf. modern Arabic 'bilad', town).

Pomponius Mela refers to Tripoli as *Oea oppidum* ('the town of Oea' – Latin). Strabo or a later copyist mistakenly wrote *Eoa* for *Oea*.

Silius Italicus called the Phoenician settlement *Trinacrios Afris permixta colonos*, which is a Latin phrase describing the place as being colonised by Sicilians: *coloni trinacrii*, who would have been Phoenicians already abroad, not native Sicilians. Another useful coin reads C.A.O.A.F., or *Colonia Antoniniana Oea Augusta Felix*. We know that Leptis was raised to the rank of *colonia* ('colony' – Latin) under Trajan, and it seems likely, from its Antonine title, that Tripoli was similarly elevated shortly afterwards.

To sum up, the name has probably passed through four major phases: Libyan *Uiat* – Latin *Oea* – medieval *Aias* – modern Tripoli – Trabulus. I am inclined to the notion that the earliest phase of all was a compound of two parts, the first being *Ait* or *Uiat* ('tribe(s)' – Libyan), and the second having disappeared, rather as though 'Suffolk' were to be represented only by the 'folk' element, the main part 'suf' (indicating 'southern') having vanished.

The establishment of Oea was favoured by two principal geographic advantages: a small natural harbour, and the presence of sufficient water to permit the existence of a permanent oasis. Silius Italicus may well be right in attributing a Siculo-African origin to present Tripoli, but its first mention in the literature is during the early Empire, when it was certainly less wealthy and powerful than Leptis.

Halfway through the second century, Apuleius – author of the *Golden Ass* – sheds intriguing light on local names in his *Apologia* against the serious charge of using magic to obtain the hand of a rich widow of Oea. His trial and the growth of his legend are described in my *Apuleius on Trial at Sabratha* (1968).

The secular history of Tripoli is then virtually unknown to us until the fourth century, the period of the Austurian depredations (363-5) and of the Tomb of Aelia Arisuth in Gargaresh oasis south of the coastal road between kilometres 5 and 6.

The Christian history of Oea is recorded from 256, when the city was represented by a bishop at the Congress of Carthage, until the end of the fifth century.

It seems likely that the Roman walls of Oea were destroyed by the Vandals between 455 and 468, when Heraclius captured for the Eastern Roman Empire the cities that the Vandals themselves had rendered helpless. Within three years, however, Heraclius withdrew from Tripoli and the Vandals renewed their occupation, despite persistent raids by tribesmen of the interior.

The Byzantines finally took Vandal possessions in North Africa in 534, but their hold was weak and lasted only until Arab armies, led by Amr ibn al-As, arrived in Tripolitania in 642-3.

Here is the story of the first Arab seizure of Tripoli, translated from at-Tijani's account of his journey across Tunisia and Tripolitania in 706-8 A.H., equivalent to 1306-9 A.D.

'The first conquest of Tripoli occurred in 22 A.H. [642-3 A.D.] and was accomplished by Amr ibn al-As, after the submission of Egypt. Having marched on Tripoli at the head of his troops, Amr camped on a small hill to the seat of the city. After a month he was no nearer to taking the town than when he arrived as a result of the vigorous resistance put up by the city's inhabitants, and the help brought to the besieged by the Nefusi Berbers.

'A soldier of Amr who belonged to the tribe of Beni Mudalaji – having left the camp one day with some companions to hunt on the western side of the besieged city – noticed, on approaching the shore, that the sea lapped the city at one point (the walls not extending as far as that) so that ships anchored in the harbour could touch the houses.

'When Amr's soldier saw that the sea, ebbing slightly, left sufficient dry land to afford access to the city, he led his companions into the heart of the city. The Greeks panicked on seeing them, some fleeing in the ships at anchor nearby, and Amr, seeing the abrupt flight of his enemies from his lookout position on the hill, was able to take advantage of the disturbance to attack the city with his troops and finally to take it.'

Since the Arabs used Tripoli as their military and administrative capital during the next centuries, their buildings naturally replaced and covered those of earlier periods, eradicating or concealing most of those indications of Roman rule which can be seen at the abandoned sites of other cities of the *treis poleis* – Leptis and Sabratha. But five of Tripoli's classical monuments have survived in part. The most impressive is the Triumphal Arch of Marcus Aurelius. The Islamic walls which even now run from Bab al-Jadid (Newgate) to a little way beyond Shar'a al-Kabira (Big Street) are almost certainly built on the ruins of Roman walls. Pottery kilns have been discovered under what is now the power station. A complex of foundation walls and sandstone platforms with mosaic fragments and Corinthian columns below the Castle seems to indicate the presence of public baths. The fifth evidence of Roman occupation is the four columns at the corners of Arb'a 'Arsat, near Bab al-Bahr.

For those accustomed to town-plans of Roman cities, a *cardo* can be detected from the Arch of Marcus Aurelius to Bab al-Hurria (Liberty Gate), a *decumanus* from the Arch along Shar'a Hara al-Kabira, and a second *decumanus* down the combined length of Shar'a al-Harrara and Shar'a Humt Garian.

5
Islam

Sundays are working days for most people in Tripoli, but both Muslim
and foreign residents make up for this by taking a holiday on Friday
(in Arabic *yaum al-jum'a*, or 'the day of gathering-together') which is
celebrated in a *jam'a* (mosque, or 'place of gathering-together'). As a
reverent non-Muslim, I have been allowed to attend the Imam's private
seminary on the *Qur'an* in the Mosque of Ahmad Pasha Caramanli.
We sat cross-legged at the feet of the seated teacher, a passage being
read aloud in turn by each pupil – normally a man of mature age, since
school-children are taught the Qur'an in school.

The *Qur'an* is the infallible word of Allah, revealed by stages to the
Prophet Muhammad (salla Allahu'alayhi wa sallam) by the Angel
Gabriel. As a transcript of a tablet preserved in Heaven, the *Qur'an* is
considered apart from all other books. It must never rest under other,
human-inspired books, nor must it be touched with the left hand,
which is considered unclean. No-one ignorant of the history and the
five principles of Islam (the word means 'surrender', with the implica-
tion 'to the will of Allah') can possibly understand the customs of
Libya, far less the attitude of Libyan friends he will talk to and observe.

The five pillars of the faith are profession, prayer, fasting, alms, and
pilgrimage. Islam demands of its adherents a profession of faith (*tashah-
hud*) that 'There is no god but Allah (and) Muhammad is the prophet
of Allah'. In Arabic this resounds mightily: *la ilahu ill' Allah: Muham-
madun rasul Ullah*. Ritual prayer (*salat*) must be accomplished five times
a day, facing Mecca. The faithful are called from the minaret of every
mosque with the muezzin's cry: '*Allahu akbar. Allahu akbar. Ashhadu
anna la ilahu ill' Allah. Ashhadu anna Muhammadan rasul Ullah. Ashhadu
anna la ilahu ill' Allah. Ashhadu anna Muhammadan rasul Ullah.*'

The muezzin concludes by calling 'God is almighty. God is almighty. There is no god but Allah.'

It is compulsory for all Muslims to attend the second, noon, prayer of Friday in his local mosque. Before praying he washes his hands, face, arms, head, ears, neck and feet, and puts on clean clothes. After washing (which in the desert may be accomplished with sand instead of precious water), the Muslim touches the lobes of his ears with his thumbs and pronounces *Allahu akbar* ('God is almighty') followed by the *suratu 'l-fatiha* (opening chapter) of the *Qur'an*: a piece of ecclesiastical music no less impressive than a Bach cantata.

Bismillahi ar-rahmani 'r-rahim,	In the name of Allah, the Compassionate, the Merciful,
al-hamdu lillahi rabbi 'l-alamin,	Praise be to Allah, Lord of the Creation,
ar-rahmani 'r-rahim,	The Compassionate, the Merciful,
maliki yaumi 'd-din,	King of the Last Judgement!
iyyaka na'budu wa iyyaka nasta 'in,	You alone we worship, and to You alone we pray for help.
ihdina as-sirat al-mustaqim,	Lead us in the straight way, The way of those whom You have favoured,
sirat alladhina an'amta 'alaihim,	Not of those who have incurred Your wrath
ghairi 'l-maghdubi wa la ad-dalin. Amin.	Nor of those who have gone astray. Amen.

The third pillar of Islam is fasting (*saum*), which is undertaken from dawn to sunset by every able-bodied Muslim during the twenty-nine or thirty days of the ninth month (Ramadan) of the lunar Muslim year. The fourth obligation is a legal tithe (*zakat*) as distinct from voluntary alms-giving and the customary alms given at the breaking of the fast. The fifth and final pillar of Islam is the pilgrimage (*hajj*) to Mecca and Medina entitling the returning pilgrim to the honourable addition of Haj before his name.

In Tripoli the pillars of the faith stand sturdily and enduring. The nights of Ramadan are a-bustle with social visits and tempting meals before the dawn abstention. Religious endowments (*awqaf*) thrive as never before. A grandiose new mosque – the biggest in Libya – is being built opposite the Government Hospital in the street aptly named after the Grand Sanusi – Muhammad bin 'Ali.

Sudden prosperity has brought to thousands the blessed prospect of visiting the holy places of Saudi Arabia on the *hajj*: formerly a privilege of the wealthy few.

Secular holidays in Tripoli are fixed according to the Gregorian calendar: March 22 – Arab League anniversary; April 26 – Unification Day; August 9 – Armed Forces Day; November 21 – United Nations Resolution Day; December 24 – Independence Day.

Islamic holidays are, of course, movable: visitors intending to do business must enquire beforehand. The Government recognises as holidays the first and second days of the month of Shawwal ('*Id al-Fitr*); the first and second of Dhu 'l-Hija ('*Id al-Adha*); the Islamic New Year, which falls on the first of Muharram; the tenth of Muharram; the twelfth of Rabi' al-Awwal; the twenty-sixth of Rajab; and the fourteenth of Sha'aban. Holidays that would fall on a weekly day of rest are observed on the day before or after the rest day.

6
Mosques

Permits to visit mosques in Tripoli on all days except Friday can be obtained at no cost from the Tourist Office near the Gazelle Fountain.

Jam'a Sidi Hammuda

One of the oldest in Tripoli, the mosque of Sidi Hammuda is inconspicuously placed between Jaddat Istiqlal and Maidan ash-Shuhada. Little is known of Sidi Hammuda himself except a few words in the *Isharat* of Shaikh Abdussalam al-Alam at-Tajuri, mentioning that Sidi Hammuda was 'one of the most recent exalted ones', or mystics. The earliest religious building on the site was founded by and named for a grandmother (*jadda* in Arabic) of an Aghlabite ruler of Ifriqia (comprising Tunisia and the Three Cities of Tripolitania) and later became known as the *Jam'a al-Barzi*, after the learned Abu 'l-Hasan al-Barzi, who resided there.

The Turkish governor Mustafa Pasha renovated the mosque in 1269 A.H. (corresponding to 1852 A.D.), and it was during his governorate that the first shops were built around it and around the cemetery behind the mosque. The cemetery was demolished in the mid-1930s to make the square opposite the castle walls more spacious after the mosque had undergone its latest reconstruction, in a neo-Moorish style, in 1923.

The best pedestrian approach to the Old City, where the chief mosques are located, is down Jaddat Istiqlal. Cross Maidan as-Saraya and pass the bronze statue of Septimius Severus on your right before entering Suq al-Mushir where sheepskin vendors gather.

27

Jam'a Ahmad Pasha Caramanli

Ahmad Pasha was founder of the Caramanli dynasty who ruled Tripoli from 1711 to 1835. The family came from Caraman (or Karaman), a town near Konya in Turkey which was the capital of the medieval kingdom of Karamania until the Ottoman Turks overcame its resistance in the fifteenth century.

Ahmad came to Tripoli as a captain in the Turkish Corps of Chivalry: his ambition, courage and popularity with the Tripolitans embittered the Governor, who practised the ancient device (it occurs even in *Hamlet*) of sending his enemy on a mission to a tribal chief bearing his sealed death warrant. But Ahmad learned of the nature of the letter and stopped in Suq al-Jum'a, where he raised an army of Cologhlis and attacked Tripoli successfully, proclaiming himself Regent in 1711 at the age of 25.

In the early period of his rule, Tripoli enjoyed prosperity. The present Great Mosque was begun in 1149 A.H. (1736 A.D.) on the site of the Jam'a ad-Diwan, the last of a glorious tradition of religious buildings going back to the original Islamic conquest in the seventh century. Part of its courtyard is a burial ground for members of the Caramanli family, including the founder himself, his heir Hassan Bey (who was murdered by his younger brother Yusuf Pasha) and Yusuf the fratricide. To the right of the courtyard the visitor can see the stone washbasins used before praying, and the entrance to the old religious school.

The interior of the mosque is a place of total silence and peace, contrasting vividly with the commotion in Suq al-Mushir.

Visitors of either sex and of any religion may enter and look around the mosque. Quietness is a necessary courtesy, of course, and one must remove one's shoes (the stone floors are carpeted) before inspecting the airy hall with its sixteen marble columns of the Islamic Baroque supporting a domed and stuccoed ceiling. The walls glitter with blue, yellow and green geometric tiles bearing Quranic inscriptions. The *mihrab* – a niche indicating the direction of Mecca – is cut in the eastern walls. The Imam leads daily prayers while standing in front of the *mihrab* and beside the *minbar*, or pulpit, from which the Friday sermon is delivered.

The ornate stucco work throughout the mosque is of North African workmanship, while the decorative ensemble is of the Southern Mediterranean School, founded by Andalusian craftsmen driven out of Spain after the Reconquest.

Jam'a an-Naqa

Returning from the Jam'a Ahmad Pasha into Suq al-Mushir, one turns right into Suq al-Attara (Spice Market) which belies its ancient name by its hospitality to numerous jewellers, and at the Freedom Café at the end of Suq al-Attara one bears right again into Suq as-Siagha (Goldsmiths' Market), reaching after a hundred metres – on the left – a tiny mosque that has the reputation of being, in foundation, the first in Tripoli: Jam'a an-Naqa, or Mosque of the She-Camel. It was destroyed in 1510 during a naval bombardment, and in 1610 the governor Safar Dey reconstructed a smaller mosque with some of the original materials, restoring too its ancient name.

Jam'a al-Kharruba

Immediately opposite the Camel Mosque is the Jam'a al-Kharruba (Carob-Tree Mosque – a small mosque with carob-trees nowhere near. This is how the name was given to it.

Among the numerous epidemics in its long history, Tripoli suffered one (probably typhoidal) which affected the digestive system: the onset of the disease was indicated by red spots which began to appear around the navel and gradually covered the body. Those attacked by the plague very soon died. Families shut themselves up from the danger of infection, never daring to go outdoors. Still the epidemic spread, until it was decreed that immediately the dreaded red spots appeared on a Tripolitan's body, he was condemned to leave the city and walk beyond its boundaries to the distance of an arrow-shot. To begin with, the expelled found fruit and vegetables to eat outside the city walls, but when their numbers increased, those who were slow to die could find nothing but the fleshy pods of carobs growing wild in a wood

where the Zawiat al-Kharruba later stood – near the Government
Hospital in Shar'a as-Saidi.

But those who were reduced to chewing carob pods for sustenance
did not die: they actually improved in health to the point where they
were considered cured. Although medicine now recognises a carob
ingredient as useful against intestinal diseases, the Tripolitans of that
period naturally regarded their salvation as a miracle. Inside the walls
of Tripoli only one carob tree existed, and as soon as the inhabitants
realised its curative properties it was plundered of pods, leaves and
even bark – the legends say that the roots were clawed up and devoured
by those too weak to snatch at a pod. The plague soon petered out. In
gratitude to the wonderful powers of the tree, the people erected a
mosque where the carob had stood, very near to the Jam'a an-Naqa.

Jam'a Sidi Abdulwahhab

The Arch of Marcus Aurelius stands at its original level below and
between two mosques. The larger is that built by Mustafa Gurgi, and
the smaller, on the site of the gateway of Oea's port, that dedicated to
Shaikh Sidi Abdulwahhab, who is buried there. In his *Travels* of
706-708 A.H. (corresponding to 1306-1309 A.D.), at-Tijani honours
the holy Abdulwahhab, who wrote a book describing his visions of the
Prophet (salla Allahu 'alayhi wa sallam) and is reputed never to have
acted without consulting Him. Muslims departing on the pilgrimage
to Mecca traditionally say their last prayers on Libyan soil in this
mosque.

Jam'a Gurgi

The minaret of the Gurgi mosque is as beautiful a work of Islamic
architecture as any to be found in Libya. The mosque was begun in
1249 (equivalent to 1833 A.D.) by the scion of a family originally from
Georgia – hence *Gurgi* in Arabic. Yusuf Caramanli, the younger son
of the Ahmad Pasha who built the Great Mosque in Suq al-Mushir,
befriended the sealord Mustafa Gurgi and even offered him one of his
daughters in marriage. So the legend of the Gurgi mosque's foundation may well be based on fact.

As Yusuf Pasha and Gurgi were watching the corsair ships conducting captured vessels into Tripoli harbour, Yusuf's satisfaction was so great that he offered Gurgi the last in the convoy of eight ships. Gurgi the corsair was responsible for the catch, and the Pasha was aware of the extent of his good fortune. But as the last of the line was traditionally loaded very lightly to assist quick pursuit of escaping captives, the Pasha felt sure that the bulk of the booty would be distributed principally between the other seven. In the event he was completely wrong: the last ship carried most of the pirate's treasure and, to avoid Yusuf Pasha's wrath, Mustafa Gurgi offered to build a mosque with his ptofirs.

Situated behind the Arch of Marcus Aurelius, high above the ancient level of the Roman Forum, the Gurgi mosque is Hanafi in plan. Like the Caramanli mosque it has no courtyard facing the prayer hall, but only vestibules flanking the main body of the building. Mustafa and his family are buried at the side.

The vestibules and interior walls are all decorated with tiles of geometric stellar designs, leaves and other floral scenes of possibly Persian derivation. Complete sequences of tiles illustrating Islamic rites adorn the outer wall of the prayer hall. These are Tunisian workmanship; similar scenes are found in Kairouan mosques.

The main hall is full of interest: marble columns, excellent stucco, decorated walls and an abundance of colour – red, blue, yellow and green.

In no Tripoli mosque, however, will you ever see a fresco, mosaic, or sculpture of any living creature. According to one interpretation, the Qur'an prohibits such representations as severely as it prohibits usury, since creation is for Allah alone. It is believed that at the Last Judgment He will challenge the artists to make their works live and condemn those unable to do so. (This prohibition does not extend to films shown in Tripoli, which are either produced in the Arab world, or are given subtitles in Arabic.)

Islam has produced great art, nevertheless. Many Persian miniatures include exquisite portraits, and the magnificence of arabesque (the name is significant) in sculpture and paint have distinguished countless buildings in the Arab world. If Muslim art has by its very nature been unable to produce a Tintoretto or a Renoir, then it can claim the Alhambra of Granada, the great mosques of Cairo, the Taj Mahal, and countless other architectural marvels of detail and grandeur from Moorish Spain to the Indies.

1 Tripoli during the Spanish domination (1510–1530). A Venetian engraving of 1567.

2   Tripoli besieged by the French in 1685, showing the moat surrounding the city.

3 Tripoli in the mid-eighteenth century. An artist's impression.

4   Ladies of Tripoli. Eighteenth-century Italian engraving.

5   The Old City in the 1920's, with the Caramanli Mosque in the centre foreground.

6 Suq al-Mushir in 1919, during the Italian period.

7 Jam'a an-Naqa
minaret.

8 Tripoli Harbour from the Yacht Club, the Castle in the right background.

9   Makhzan ar-Rakham: Gurgi minaret and Roman temple relief.

10   Makhzan ar-Rakham: Arch of Marcus Aurelius and the *funduqs* (left and right).

7
The Old City

Tripoli *was* the Old City until the twentieth-century: the enchanting
*Letters written during a ten years' (July 1783-August 1793) residence at the
Court of Tripoli,* by Miss Tully, sister of the British Consul, narrate life
in the narrow lanes – so sinister in those days – beyond which were the
city walls, still standing to the south-west, and then the oasis of Tripoli
and the empty desert. Miss Tully lived in Shar'a al-Kuwash 27, still
standing behind the Gurgi Mosque. Some administrative buildings and
a Government Hospital stood outside the city walls, but it was only
after the Turks were driven out that Tripoli began to expand. The
main thoroughfares were no longer Suq at-Turk, Shar'a al-Hara
al-Kabira, and Suq al-Mushir, but the arteries radiating from Maidan
as-Saraya (Castle Square) east – now Shar'a Adrian Pelt; south-west –
Jaddat 'Umar al-Mukhtar; and, fanlike to the south-east, Shar'a Amr
ibn al-As, Shar'a Mizran, Shar'a 24 December (leading to Shar'a Jam'a
Magharba), Jaddat Istiqlal, and Shar'a al-Baladia.

The topography of Tripoli can best be mastered by ascending the
Castle to the very summit (it is open every day (9-12 and 3-6) and its
museums are of the greatest interest), and looking out from the cannon
heights over the port east to the Ceremonial Jetty, the minaret of the
Jam'a Sidi Billimam, and as far as the huge Caramanli Mole. The
bell-tower of the Roman Catholic Cathedral is then visible to the south,
with the Royal Palace domes behind it.

To the north is the busy port, which nevertheless seldom seems to
lose the tranquillity of summer evenings, even in the hectic period of
the Tripoli International Fair, held annually in March.

The plan of the old city as we see it nowadays is pentagonal, the
longest side being the harbour frontage from the Castle to the docks,

and the shortest the south-easterly castle wall that forms a right angle
to Shar'a Adrian Pelt and the first stretch of Jaddat 'Umar al-Mukhtar.

In his Arabic *Chronicle of Tripoli*, the eighteenth-century historian
Ibn Ghalbun, who was born in Misurata, characterises the old city of
Tripoli as 'a charming town with a good climate and citizens who are
endowed with courage and steadfastness, following the tenets of Islam
as closely as the first Companions of the Prophet (salla Allahu 'alayhi
wa sallam). It is a place gracious of aspect and ample of proportion,
the equilibrium between land and sea being such that the spirit may
find repose. Allah has rained blessings on its people, who love all that
come to live among them. Its beauty is enhanced by the Manshia
[the oasis of Tripoli that extended at that time from the city gates
towards Mellaha], which in its lovely views and fertility recalls the
Garden of Paradise. The sea surrounds it at east and west: its position
in the sea is like that of the centre of a heart. The varieties of its fruit
are beyond computation.'

Whenever I enter Tripoli's old city I experience an odd sensation
that might be rather akin to that of a bucket dropping down a well:
darkness, narrowness, surprise. Suq al-Mushir (the Marshal's Market,
the marshal concerned being Rajab Pasha) is perhaps the most evoca-
tive entrance – by a breach in the castle walls.

If you go down to the Artisans' Market left of Suq al-Mushir any
morning of the week except Friday, between eight and nine, you will
be able to buy great skeins of wool at an informal women's market that
is also a vital, if little-known, part of Tripoli's local atmosphere. One
of the wool-sellers also makes charming dolls in Libyan national dress
for L£1.750. Wool is sold by the kilogram at about 750 milliemes: an
official weigher will ensure that you are given the precise amount of
wool you pay for. This wool-market, in contrast to the lively camel
fair at Suq al-Jum'a, lasts no longer than an hour: the women have
disappeared by nine, when the men come to pull up the shutters of
their shops.

The white brilliance of walls, roofs and slender minarets is one of the
first attractions for a European: at-Tijani could call Tripoli 'the white

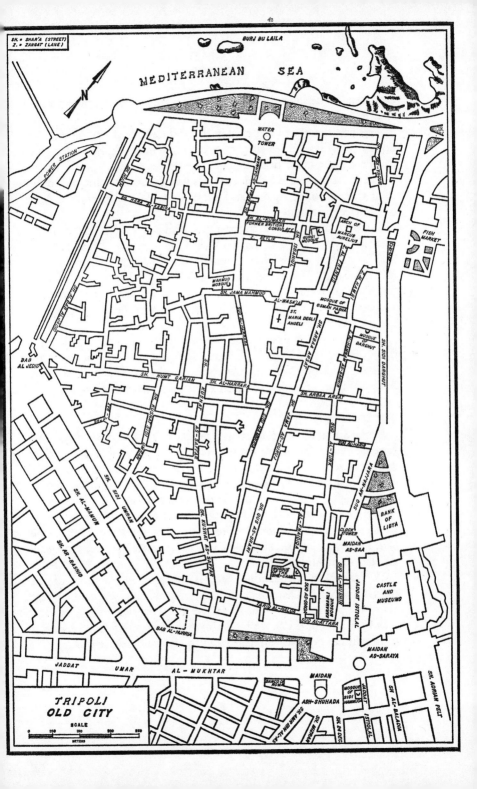

city' even in the fourteenth century. Palms thrive even in this narrow-streeted quarter.

Here and there, and not only in the Old City, high on the walls of houses you will see dried eucalyptus leaves, an insect-repellent, hanging from nails like faded bridal bouquets.

The great sea, often a deep blue in summer, can be glimpsed to the right when strolling up Suq at-Turk towards al-Was'aia and the Arch of Marcus Aurelius.

Opposite the Roman arch are a new Fish Market (on the site of an ancient predecessor) and *Tripoli Yacht Club – Private, Members Only*, near a modern sports club. Behind them all is the mosque of Haj Mustafa Gurgi. The crossroads of the Old City, running parallel with Suq at-Turk, is the Arb'a 'Arsat (Four Columns), at which the curious will not only find a Roman column set in each of the four angles, but exquisite Corinthian capitals surviving on two of them.

The Old City, with its numerous culs-de-sac and winding alleys, is the original site of Tripoli. Evidence has been provided not only by coins and inscriptions, but also by the excavation from deep sand of the Arch of Marcus Aurelius, situated at the original jetty of Oea.

The Roman Arch

Bernard Berenson wrote in his Tripoli diary for May 19, 1955: *In a horse-cab through the whole length of the town to the quadrifrontal Arch of Marcus Aurelius. Had forgotten how complete the stone cupola is and how dignified and noble the figures of prisoners in the remaining but fast disintegrating reliefs. From there we wander through the oldest quarter of the town. Neither in the souks of Cairo or of Aleppo or of Damascus have I had such an impression of exotic Orient and remoteness from the West as in the souk here. Picturesque and paintable in the style of Delacroix and Decamps and all the other Orientalizing artists.*

The enduring, elephantine Arch is the principal element of the Roman Forum of Oea which still lies, unexcavated, seven to ten feet below the present level of the Old City. It was divested of its shops and accumulated rubble in 1913 by Ghislanzoni, whose efforts to excavate further in the Forum were frustrated by the outbreak of war.

Caius Calpurnius Celsus, an affluent Roman magistrate, paid for the Arch to be erected at the entrance to the harbour where the two main streets of Oea intersected. The work of Greek masons, it was dedicated in 163 A.D. to the emperors Marcus Aurelius and Lucius Verus.

Below Winged Victories on the south-west aspect appear the tripod and raven of Apollo, on the left, and Minerva's helmet, shield, spear, and owl on the right. Apollo and Minerva are the patron deities of Oea, and appear in person on the fragment of the pediment of a Temple situated near the Arch and roughly contemporary with it. The fragment, to be found in the north-western area of the Arch Square (Makhzan ar-Rukham), shows Oea's Goddess of Good Fortune in the centre, flanked by Apollo, who leans on the Delphic tripod, and helmeted, warlike Minerva.

The British Consuls' Former Residence

Behind the Gurgi Mosque, in Shar'a al-Kuwash (Baker Street) bakers at open-air ovens wield long wooden shovels, depositing their crisp yellow loaves beside the white dough moulds awaiting their turn.

The baker works below ground level, so that the street becomes his counter. The cry *Barlik, Barlik* warns passers-by of the emerging loaves now as it did in 1744 when the Caramanli family built the palace, later to be presented for use as the residence for the British Consul.

The small doorway is deceptive: inside, an ample courtyard leads to a staircase, and a graceful loggia looks out on the courtyard. Uniformed lackeys flanked the flight of steps on a visitor's entrance, and a bodyguard always hovered near at hand, for this was a foreigners' sanctuary in Barbary.

Successive British Consuls-General lived in the historic building until the 1920s, when Italian colonial rule had reduced British prestige in Tripolitania. The palace was sold to an Italian resident for £2,000. Now Cav. Mario Fabbri, attached to the Prehistory Museum in Tripoli Castle, lives in the upper floor of the historic building, and the remaining rooms (formerly offices, kitchens and servants' quarters) are let to other foreign residents. After water-pipe flooding, the structure is showing signs of collapse into softening ground, and wooden supports have been lodged across the alley to prevent sudden disintegration. A spiral staircase ascends past the loggia to a wide terrace, with a particularly good view of the Gurgi minaret – and views west to the former French consulate in Zanqat al-Fransis 32, and south to S. Maria degli Angeli, the cathedral of Tripoli until 1928.

From this terrace the astronomer husband of Mabel Loomis Todd studied eclipses of the sun in 1900 and 1905, while Mabel herself spent her time travelling and writing about *Tripoli the mysterious* (London: Grant Richards, 1911). In her day, Tripoli had no tourists; there was no city outside the walls at all. 'Camels were decidedly the best conconveyance to go by' on her jaunts to the caves of Gargaresh 'but one time we had excellent donkeys for the trip'.

Mabel Todd adored Tripoli with all the passion of her poetry-starved Massachusetts upbringing. She loved the black, starry nights buzzing with the conference of wind and sea and the proximity of the desert. She loved its Roman Arch and Islamic minarets. On returning to the States she wrote: '(Tripoli) remains quiescent in the sense of world progress, but its charm was never to be resisted. A city of enchantment white as dreams of Paradise.'

But the woman who will be remembered most vividly by the visitor to Shar'a al-Kuwash 27 is Emma Laing, the daughter of the British Consul Hanmer Warrington. Gordon Laing was a Scots explorer who determined to reach Timbuktu from Tripoli, and while making his preparations he and Emma fell in love, despite the Consul's apprehensions about the future happiness of a girl tied to a daredevil like Laing. Warrington, finally persuaded, wrote back to London in his report dated 14 July 1925, *Although I am aware that Major Laing is a very Gentlemanly, honorable and good Man still I must allow a more Wild, Enthusiastic and Romantic Attachment never before existed and consequently every Remonstrance, every Argument, & every feeling of disapprobation was resorted to by me to prevent even an Engagement under the existing circumstance the disadvantages so evidently appearing to attach to my Daughter.*

After a Voluminous correspondence, I found my wishes, exertions, Entreaties, and displeasure, quite futile & of no avail, under all circumstances, both for the Public good, as well as their Mutual happiness, I was obliged to consent to Perform the Ceremony, under the most Sacred, & most Solemn Obligation that they are not to cohabit till the Marriage is duly performed by a Clergyman of the established Church of England, and as my honor is so much involved, that I shall take due care they never be one Second from under the observation of myself or Mrs Warrington.

On 10 November 1826, Emma heard that Laing had reached Timbuktu, despite having been attacked by Tuareg in the Hoggar mountains, and left at the point of death. *Why let me deceive myself,* she wrote to him, *with the hopes of your speedy return? The month I first expected you to return is passed away, & disappointed & sickened I looked forward to the next but to be disappointed again. At last the dreadful truth was revealed to me & without being at all prepared for it the blow was most severe. I heard of your wounds, of your sickness – the chill of death appeared to pass over me. Not a word, not a complaint could I utter – not a tear would fall from my eyes to relieve the agonising oppression of my heart. I spent the whole night in a state of stupefaction, not understanding anything I heard.*

Returning from Timbuktu, Laing was ambushed again, mutilated, and decapitated. But Emma had no news of him until August 1828, when she finally understood that her husband was dead. To assuage her grief, Warrington induced her to marry again (Thomas Wood, the British Vice-Consul in Benghazi), but less than six months later she herself died. The general opinion was that her health had been broken in Tripoli: but this is the story of a broken heart.

8
Historic Houses

No evidence remains, apart from a few additions made haphazardly to the Castle, of architecture of the Christian period, dominated by Spain and Malta, before the Turkish conquest of 1551. It is during the second half of the sixteenth century that Tripoli turns from a settlement into a city, vital and bustling with commercial activity. The wealthy merchants and administrators began to consider their houses as places of elegance and relaxation, rather than refuges in a storm, and from the end of the sixteenth century to the beginning of the nineteenth the patrician houses of Tripoli sprang up in modest profusion.

The Turkish rulers strengthened the castle and city fortifications, and rebuilt mosques, baths, and shops. Above all, the aspect of the Old City that we see today is predominantly Turkish, a marvellous ensemble of history and beauty worthy of the most careful preservation.

Although only the Mahsin house built in 1228 A.H. (1813 A.D.) by Yusuf al-Khamayyir is dated and signed, it is always possible in other cases to establish a rough date, and thus a rough chronology of the main periods, by noting the styles and decorative forms – and comparing these with the styles of mosques known to be contemporary – as well as hints given up by the archives of the houses themselves. The lack of trained architects and builders in this outpost of the Turkish Empire led to a duplication of function: the same artists worked on mosques and private houses when called upon. Motifs and forms were repeated, with minimal changes, from generation to generation, some remaining virtually unchanged from 1600 to 1800, and others changing slowly or gradually disappearing. So the division of Tripolitan houses of the Turkish period into three phases proceeds not so much by an analysis of the overall construction, but by the recognition of certain details in the decoration.

The first, most ancient, phase is that from 1551 to the end of the seventeenth century, including the baths of Sidi Darghut of 1013 A.H. (1604-5 A.D.) and the mosque of Muhammad Pasha Sha'ib al-'Ain of 1110 A.H. (1698-9 A.D.) in Suq at-Turk.

The second and third groups are less distinctive, both belonging to the period of Yusuf Caramanli, from 1795 to 1832. These two groups are easily confused, and may be differentiated only by certain elements which relate the second group to the mosque of Ahmad Pasha Caramanli (1148-1150 A.H. or 1735-1737 A.D.), and the third group to the mosque of Mustafa Gurgi (1249 A.H., or 1833 A.D.). The similarities between the three groups are obvious; the differences are subtle, discovered here in a detail of the construction, and there in a decorative feature.

Possibly more than any other Oriental city, Tripoli reveals a close affinity with Roman domestic models: an open central patio surrounded by colonnades, often with a basin (or *impluvium*) to catch the rain, with rooms leading off all four walls. The only variations from this norm are the houses of the wealthier citizens, who prefer a more complex design, perhaps adding a smaller patio elsewhere, to divide the house into the owner's (male) quarters, and the female quarters. As a rule the owner possesses one large room (*ghurfat as-saqifa*) entered directly from the patio or from the street.

The square patio is virtually the centre of the house. Access to it from the street is obtained by means of a small dividing corridor. The women of the house spend much of their time in the patio, and retire to their own quarters if the master of the house enters with a stranger. A veranda often looks out from the first floor over the patio. In the earlier houses – those of the first group – a ground-floor portico is confined to one side of the patio, normally the side of the entrance, and the stairway opens on the opposite side of the patio. Later on, the ground-floor portico extends to all four sides. The earliest houses have columns of local pink marble, probably from Garian or Azizia. Later on, these columns are of wood. The most recent houses have columns of white marble imported from Italy.

The styles of capitals on the patio columns have evolved from absolute, almost geometrical simplicity, in the case of the first group, though occasional leaf-designs are encountered, to the characteristic Tripolitan leaf-design found everywhere in the second period: in both public and private buildings, on the external portico of the Caramanli mosque, and indeed in numerous houses otherwise devoid of decoration. The leaf, bizarrely reminiscent of the canthus that swirls up the columns of the Severan basilica at Leptis, is repeated at each corner of the capital. The capitals of the third period lose their local flavour, and reproduce the Italianate influence of the marble. These early nineteenth-century artists made one concession to the Libyan environment: they simply incorporated a crescent! In every other particular the architectural style is occidental and undistinguished.

The Tripolitan arch is not the Roman arch, an example of which can be seen in Makhzan ar-Rakham; nor is it the Arab arch familiar in Kairouan or Cordova. It is a compromise between the two.

Windows and doors of rooms overlooking the patio are generally limited to one on each of the four sides; the rooms do not intercommunicate. The rooms are consequently proportionately long, even luxuriously so. At each end of a room there is a raised platform called a *sedda*, curtained for use as a bed. Between the two, the space is used as a reception area for guests.

But, like all oriental houses, the house of Tripoli is less important for its overall proportions and design than for its brilliant decoration: stucco, tiles, intarsia, marble, painted wooden ceilings. . . . Sculptured ledges are found only in the earliest period, when tiles are less frequently encountered. Marble, which permits the most detailed sculpting, early on gives way to the more friable local stone. The finest arabesque decoration is that of the House of the Pashas in Shar'a Jam'a ad-Duruj, and in a pair of houses in the street called Kushat as-Saffar, all contemporary with the late seventeenth-century mosque of Muhammad Pasha in Suq at-Turk.

The rose motif is confined to a vertical line above the arch. The arabesque covers the architraves and borders and carries the weight of the decorative emphasis despite its excessively low relief. Such forms derive basically from orthodox Arab design, but there are clear echoes of the Italian art of the seventeenth century. The palms hung with dates to be seen on a house in Shar'a Kushat as-Saffar, on the other hand, display a powerfully Tripolitan bias, and compositionally offset the bunches of grapes hanging from the entwined vine bordering the door. Obviously the artist was drawing from nature (sufficiently rare at this period to be remarked) but he was also recalling the local Byzantine-Tripolitan tradition familiar to him from Leptis and elsewhere.

The wall decoration in these houses is the coloured tile, originally from the modern Iran-Iraq region, but superbly adapted by the Turks for their city of Constantinople and their North African cities. Tiles predominate in the historic houses of Tripoli much as mosaics constituted the principal decorative element in Tripolitania's Roman villas – there is the same polychrome invention, the same inherent illustrative interest that draws the eye and the mind into the design's convolutions. The houses and mosques of the earliest period are the least rich in tile ornamentation; later buildings of Tripoli use tiles in the lower section of patio walls and the walls of the more important rooms, and almost as frequently on the floors of rooms in simple chessboard or diagonal compositions of alternating white and brown. Since tiles were used as decoration almost contemporaneously everywhere in Tripoli, the style is virtually uniform. The design is usually floral, as in Istanbul mosques, consisting of repetitive roses or stars; only very occasionally docs a complex of tiles form a picture, as in Delftware, and even then the picture takes the form of a tree or bowl of flowers in which the traditional floral elements play their ordinary role.

The carved and painted wood decoration of Tripoli buildings is derived from Muslim art. Again the design is usually floral – very delicately coloured and slender of dimension. The wooden ledges round the verandas are striking in their uniformity throughout Tripoli, elegant but functional in the style of the Egyptian *mushrabia*.

While stucco is found in characteristic profusion in the city's two main mosques, few examples are to be found in private homes.

Does the Villa Volpi – a late eighteenth-century mansion built by the Caramanli dynasty – live up to its reputation as the most elegant patrician home in Tripoli? I think it does. It combines the Arab passion for fountains, vistas of gardens delightful to look at and marvellously scented, with dazzling white marble and a world-traveller's eclecticism in the contents of the house: a Thai silk wall hanging, high wicker chairs from the Philippines, brass-studded chests from Zanzibar.

A mass of bougainvillea hangs and spreads from horseshoe arch to horseshoe arch in an open courtyard off the central patio. In the middle of the courtyard Contessa Anna Maria Cicogna Volpi has sunk an elaborate stone parterre modelled on the grape garden of Akbar in Agra. The tracing, flush with the paving, has a Roman fish-scale design and among the intricate stone paths there is a field of white-starred jasmine. Beyond, a wall of mesembryanthemum covers the sides of a turquoise pool kept continuously fresh by artesian wells.

There is a trellis-tunnel of magnificent red roses. In the former harem of this house, sadly inaccessible to public view, hang fifteenth-century paintings from Crete. A tented pavilion of the Coromandel coast is worked in bright cottons. A shallow rectangular pond harbours water-lily pads and clumps of papyrus. Palms, carefully protected from the damp, rise inexplicably from the surface of the water.

A lovely building of the early 1880s is Shar'a Adrian Pelt 18. This noble house is the most distinguished example of domestic architecture in what was formerly known as the *Manshia*, now the New City. Imaginative later use of wrought iron divides the tranquil garden (now overlooked by the Libya Palace Hotel) from the elegant interior. There will always be a need for vigilance on the part of the municipal authorities to preserve and restore Tripoli's heritage of historic houses. Not only are they superb examples of Maghribi domestic architecture over several centuries of evolution, but simply as places to live in they offer the same combination of comfort and elegance that modern architects and designers often fail to achieve no matter how clearly they understand the need and attempt to fulfil it.

9
Churches

The Roman Catholic Cathedral, Maidan al-Jaza'ir

Of all the churches in Tripoli, the most grandiose – though not the most interesting – is the Roman Catholic Cathedral of the Sacred Heart of Jesus. The parish church of Funduq at-Tughar, on the Swani road, is important because of its permanent exhibition of drawings and books on Christian antiquities of Tripolitania. San Francesco, in the suburb of Dahra, has all the atmosphere of Sicily on Sunday mornings, and is a favourite for weddings in the Italian community.

But the Cathedral, designed by Panteri and inaugurated in November 1928, is a landmark for sailors; it looms over pedestrians sauntering from the Royal Palace to the Seraglio in a manner reminiscent of a Lombard *duomo* dominating its town.

The basilica, of Latin-cross design, is 54 metres long and 35 metres wide. The central nave is 11.6 metres wide, and each of the side naves 5.6 metres. The height of the central nave is 22 metres, while that of the cupola is exactly double.

Sanctuary of the Madonna della Guardia, Jaddat 'Umar al-Mukhtar

A church in the Romanesque style built by the Franciscans, with a single nave and a statue of the Madonna della Guardia, a copy of the Genoese original given in 1926 by Cardinal Minoretti, Archbishop of Genoa.

S. Maria degli Angeli

The *Was'aia* is called simply 'the square' because before the construction of the new city it was virtually the only open space in the old city's maze of narrow streets. Until the houses numbered 13-27 were built, the *Was'aia* measured 70 metres long by 50 metres wide. Its importance for the western visitor resides in its two Christian churches: the Roman Catholic Santa Maria degli Angeli, and the Greek Orthodox Hagios Georgios.

S. Maria is a neo-Gothic Franciscan church whose origins go back almost to the beginnings of Christianity in Barbary, but the first chapel on the site to be dedicated to Our Lady of the Angels was built in 1680. Others followed, the present church having been completed in 1897.

The important painting of the *Madonna with Angels* by Giuseppe Mancinelli dominates the church. It was donated by Ferdinand III, King of the Two Sicilies, to an earlier church consecrated by Padre Benedetto da S. Donato in 1829.

Mancinelli was born in Naples in 1813, and studied under Costantino Angeli at Rome. As well as his portraits (for each of which he commanded up to four hundred thalers) he was well known as a historical and religious painter, and was responsible for much of the best work on the ceiling of the Teatro di San Carlo, Naples. Mancinelli is represented in the Uffizi by a self-portrait, and in the following museums: the Municipale, Reggio; Capodimonte, Naples; Arte Moderna, Rome; as well as in churches in Naples and Sorrento, the Cathedrals of Altamura and Capua, and S. Maria del Soccorso in Capodimonte.

One need not be a connoisseur to see that Mancinelli, who died at Palazzolo Castrocielo, in the province of Caserta, on 25 March 1875, belongs more to the study of art history than to the study of art. But the absence of other important Italian paintings open to the public in Tripoli exaggerates his significance and presents him as the type of a nation's glorious art at a time when the tradition was unfortunately ebbing fast.

In this painting choirs of angels, and still higher a semi-circle of archangels, are playing musical instruments to the Virgin and Child. An idealised mid-nineteenth-century Tripoli appears in the background. The figures of S. Francesco on the left and S. Rocco on the right (with a dog between them) complete the composition which suffers from the defects of its time: sentimentality and a certain academic flatness. But Mancinelli's design has a certain power, using the expressive hands of S. Francesco to start a spiralling effect which runs up through the hands of S. Rocco into the clouds and the dominant angel on the right, then around the semi-circle of archangels to the dark robes of the Virgin (in blue, mauve and red) and the Christ child as centrepiece. The painting was begun some time before 1854, but finished only in 1857, when it was brought to Tripoli and put in the earlier church on the site in the position it now occupies on the high altar. The lower part was accidentally burned in 1870 and restored by the Maltese artist Bonnici in 1876.

Hagios Georgios

The Greek Orthodox church of St. George, dating in its present form to 1622 with restorations of 1930, serves the 1,200 Greek residents of Tripoli.

Father Anthony Antzoulidis will be glad to show you precious icons of the twelfth and thirteenth centuries. The Greek Orthodox Church teaches by pictures as well as by precept: the early Byzantine convention is that, as the shadow is close to the substance that casts it, so the picture of a saint or miracle is closely related to the physical presence of the saint, or to the reality of the miracle portrayed. The worshipper is close to the holy person or scene at whose image he gazes. To emphasise the hypnotic nature of Byzantine belief, therefore, the figures painted are nearly always shown full face. Even if the figure is shown talking to another figure in the painting, he must be shown at least three-quarter full face: only Satan, Judas Iscariot, or others among the damned, are shown in profile.

10
Tripoli Castle

The Seraglio – usually known as the Castle – represents in Tripoli's history the central position occupied by castles in mediaeval European cities, where the fortifications were generally built on the highest ground. As Tripoli is flat, and without a permanent river estuary to need guarding (the Wadi Majnin near Bab Gargaresh is filled by mountain rain only at intervals in winter), the crucial topographical defence-point is the harbour. So it was here that the Romans built their *castrum*.

Few early chronicles in Arabic and Turkish survive, but we know that in the year 819 Abdullah bin Ibrahim bin Aghlab, founder of the Aghlabite dynasty, d fended the Seraglio against his own mutinous troops and held out for over a month. In 1146 George of Antioch, an admiral in the service of Roger II of Sicily, took the Castle and held it until dispossessed by the Arabs in 1158. Fourteen years later the corsair Sharif ad-Din Qaraqush occupied Tripoli. Then in 1228, the Genoese and Venetians obtained a franchise from Abu Zakaria Yahya to trade in the Hafsite-governed area extending over eastern Algeria, Tunisia, and the port of Tripoli, in which the Italians monopolised the square of Makhzan ar-Rakham.

The Hawwara Berber adventurer Muhammad ibn Thabit took the Castle and city in 1326, but the Genoese pirate Filippo Doria established his brief rule in 1354, succeeding Muhammad's son Thabit.

As a result of the invasion of Don Pedro de Navarra, the Castle fell into the hands of the Spaniards on 25 July 1510 (by a bizarre chance the day of Santiago).

The ravages wrought by the Spaniards were such that only the Spanish garrison remained in the city: all the Tripolitans were either dead or evicted. Damage to Castle and city walls necessitated extensive reconstruction at this period, but the Castle is principally Turkish as regards its internal structure – the mosque, harems, and the courtyards still aflame with bougainvillea and silvered by cascading fountains.

Visitors entering by a small door in the Castle wall from Maidan as-Saraya (Castle Square) will first come to the Prehistory Museum on their left. Collections of artefacts and copies of rock drawings are supplemented by detailed documentation in the form of maps and charts. Opposite the Prehistory Museum is the Archaeological Museum. The vestibule is dominated by a great mausoleum from Ghirza, one of the most interesting of sites in the Tripolitanian hinterland, unfortunately accessible only by Land-Rover.

A monumental sculpture of the Emperor Claudius rules the Roman sculpture gallery as majestically as its subject reigned in life.

On the upper floor rare Roman paintings can be studied next to superb mosaics from the villa of Dar Buk Amaira (a site that can still be visited, with the less spectacular mosaics that remain) on the shore by Zliten. Possibly the most significant work of art in this section is the Scrolls Mosaic, whose composition is similar to that of the Ara Pacis in Rome. The artist is a subtle colourist with a sense of humour: watch the chameleon melt into his background while you are looking.

The Ethnographical Museum attracts western ladies because of its characteristic Libyan bridal chamber, but amply repays a more detailed examination. The Museum of Natural History deserves a visit even if one has no intention of exploring the fauna and flora of Libya personally.

Libraries of Antiquities and Natural History constitute, with the Government Library in Shar'a al-Jaza'ir, the most comprehensive collections for research on Libya in the country. The Archives in the Castle should also be mentioned in this respect: they offer original documentation from the year 1677.

Before you leave the Castle, walk up to the cannon ramparts and look over the harbour. Occasionally the noon light is hard and dazzling; much more often, however, the transparent air offers a lucid vision of things as they really are, without mist or glare. The quality of Mediterranean light has been described time and again by visitors to Greece: Tripoli's clarity is no less remarkable for being less remarked.

II
The Family

The Muslim concept of the family is not easy for anyone from a fragmented urban society to comprehend. The old saying that 'blood is thicker than water' applies to nobody more than to the Arab. Indeed, he probably invented it: *Nuqta dam wa la alf sahab* (literally 'A blood relation rather than a thousand friends'). One's interests are subject to those of one's family; the family's to the tribe's, the tribe's to the clan's. The importance of blood relationship is apt to be a little obscured, in Tripoli, by factors of migration from rural areas and social mobility within the new middle class which has risen meteorically in the ten years since prosperity from oil began to be felt in the wage-packet. This middle class consists of the new merchants (such as contractors to the various departments of an oil company), the new professional classes (such as teachers), the new administrators (such as government economists), and skilled artisans whose position is much more highly respected than it would be in a country with an artisan-class already established.

Again, it is instructive to compare the desert dweller with the townsman. In rural areas of the south, a tribe is hereditary owner of its land and elects a *shaikh* (who must be an adult male) to represent it in cases of litigation with other tribes, and claims on the government.

The secular *shaikh* and religious *imam* govern a tribal unit with the co-operation of a tribal council: together they decide family water and grazing rights, and settle disputes arising within the tribe.

The eldest male of a family performs the function of the *shaikh* within his smaller circle. As head of the family he is considered responsible for arranging marriage for his daughters and careers for his sons. He has an extraordinary degree of influence on the conduct of other

50

adult males and in return is expected to exert himself on their behalf whenever they so require.

The Tripolitan is in general rather less closely tied to his family than is the villager. But common Arab traditions of hospitality and brotherliness, and common Islamic notions of charity and faith ensure that if one has even the remotest blood-affiliations in the city he will not lack a meal and a bed. The most notable differences between townsman and villager concern the increased tempo of life and cultural awareness of the former, and the likely reduction of his family, for housing purposes, from an 'extended' group comprising the families of his brothers and sisters, to a group consisting only of himself, his wife, and his children. The Old People's Homes so essential in the West are not necessary in Tripoli, where the aged are invariably looked after with care by their younger relations.

A move to emancipate Libyan women is receiving the sympathy of the Government, and is going ahead faster in cosmopolitan Tripoli than anywhere else in Libya. Married early, a woman had until a short time ago few occupations open to her other than housewifery. Now teaching, social and secretarial work, telephone-operating, nursing, even acting are accepted ways for a woman to earn a living. The professions are becoming open to women, and the veil – still enjoined by stricter members of the older generation – is gradually being replaced by western dress. It is interesting to note, in this connection, that fewer countrywomen than townswomen adopt the veil: this is because women often help in the fields where use of the veil is simply not practicable.

12
Etiquette

The manners that make men in Tripoli owe much to Muslim tradition. But good manners are international in character, and if the visitor to Tripoli is courteous by the standards of his own home town, he will not suffer social embarrassment in Tripoli. There are, however, a few cases in which it is helpful to know the local ground rules, which change only slightly according to the social position of the individual and how well the foreign visitor knows him. They vary slightly, too, according to the number of people present, the time of day, and the place of meeting. Generally one is safer to err on the side of social conservatism than to behave in a more expansive and vocal manner.

Do not photograph women or girls, veiled or unveiled, without seeking permission through a man who may be standing nearby, and do not be aggrieved if such permission is denied. Further, when greeting a Muslim, one does not normally ask after the health of his wife or other adult female relatives unless one has met them socially.

Do not invite a Muslim to take an alcoholic drink in private or in public. Always have soft drinks at hand at home. Do not eat, drink, or smoke in public in the daytime during Ramadan, and do not ask a Muslim to do so. Do not offer pork or dishes using pork to Muslims at any time.

Do not expect a single 'No, thank you' to suffice if you are being offered a gift or food or drink. It may take several refusals, and you may find it easier to accept food and drink, and nibble or sip a little before leaving the rest. Similarly, when offering a gift or food or drink, an initial refusal is not to be taken seriously, but as a conventional politeness before acceptance. You will not be thanked effusively for any gift. Gratitude is to Allah; you are merely an agent in the giving.

In sha' Allah (If Allah wills) the sensitive visitor will soon learn the forms of politeness necessary to become more at ease in Muslim circles. Among these, variations on the use of '*In sha' Allah*' itself will become apparent. Among Muslims everywhere, however, it is appended to remarks concerning future plans or promises because the future is considered to be in the hands of Allah alone.

13
Just Talking

The official language of Libya, spoken by about 96% of the population, is Arabic, introduced by Arabs of the Beni Hilal and Beni Sulaim tribes who crossed Libya in successive waves during the seventh, ninth and eleventh centuries.

Three forms of Arabic are accepted: classical, literary and colloquial. Classical Arabic is used only by the well educated. Literary Arabic is the written and broadcast language of a status equivalent to standard English. Colloquial Arabic is used for conversational purposes and, despite local variations, can be understood from one end of the country to the other much more easily than, say, a Cornishman will understand a Glaswegian.

The Tuareg and Berber minorities who choose to retain their own language for domestic communication invariably understand Arabic.

Italian is widely spoken, but by a decreasing minority. The Italian community was 110,000 strong in 1941, but largely as a result of repatriation, the Italian population – almost entirely confined to Tripoli and the towns of Tripoli's hinterland – is reduced to 20,000, The tolerance shown by Libyans is particularly admirable in this connection, since for nearly forty years Libya was ruled by Italy, despite vigorous nationalist activity. Italians are still permitted to run their own schools and churches, and their language is understood by about 65% of Muslim Libyans over 35 years of age in the town, and by about 25% of those who live in rural areas.

English is making very rapid strides for supremacy over Italian, and within ten years of the founding of the largely U.S.-dominated oil industry in Libya, English has in fact superseded Italian as the main foreign language for doing business in Libya.

Talking is an important art in Tripoli: one can achieve far more by verbal communication, persuasion and pleading than by writing letters, memoranda, or newspaper columns. A Tripolitan will not look at the wall-posters advertising films: he is more likely to ask a friend what is on, telephone, or even walk to the cinema to find out. For his news he prefers the radio to newspapers. His attachment to the transistor is so great that I have seen soccer fans tuned in to a commentary on the game we were watching. This is not for information (he already knows the score and the players) but to experience the game more keenly.

He is sensuous and relaxed, whereas the tourist – even on holiday – is likely to be intellectual and nervous. The Tripolitan is soothed by the sound of his voice, and by those of his friends. His social conversations not only last longer than conversations about politics, religion, literature, or commerce, they are, to him, intrinsically more important.

Here is a typical swift encounter between acquaintances called Mabruk and Farid on the way to the office.

M:	Ya, Farid!	Farid!
F:	Ahlaaaan!	Good to see you!
M:	Ahlan wa sahlan!	Good to see you!
	Kaif haluk, bahi?	How are you, fine?
F:	Ahlan wa sahlan!	Good to see you!
	Kaif haluk?	How are things?
M:	Bahi, bahi. Kaif haluk?	Fine, fine. How are you doing?
F:	Al-hamdu lillah.	Praise be to God.
	Kaif hal al-aulad?	How are the kids?
M:	Kwaisin, wallahi.	Just great, thank God.
	Anta bahi?	Are you O.K.?
F:	Mish batal. Wain timshi?	Not so bad. Where are you going?
M:	Ila 'sh-sharika.	To the office.
F:	Bahi. Kaif as-sahha?	Fine. Are you well?
M:	Kwaisa.	Yes, indeed.
F:	Ma'a 's-salama.	Peace be with you.
M:	F' aman 'llah.	Adieu. (Into God's care.)

The courtesy of Libyans is legendary. If you are lost, you will be accompanied to your destination. If you venture a word to a stranger in a café, friendship will be sealed within ten minutes, just talking.

14
Eating

Visitors seeking a change from hotel cooking can try Greek food at the *Akropol* (in Cathedral Square) the *Parthenon* (Shooting and Fishing Club) or the new *Zorba*, Italian dishes at the *Delfino* (Shar'a 24 December) the nearby *Romagna* (Galleria de Bono) or the *Riviera Beach* (near the Beach Club); Tunisian and French food at *Le Paris*; Lebanese food at the *Caravan:* or American specialities at the *Chicken on Wheels* or the *Swan*, all in Giorgimpopoli.

Those on a limited budget will find the best value for money at the *Hollywood Grill* – with the best past ain town – in Shar'a 24 December.

The adventurous will want to try oriental cuisine. I suggest the *Baghdad* (Shar'a Rashid 16), where an average meal costs 750 mills, with a 10% service charge. Open from 7.30 a.m. until midnight, this is very conveniently placed to conclude a half-day walk in the Old City. The speciality of the house is a piquant lamb dish called *rishdat kaskas*, on the menu twice a week. Authentic Libyan *kuskus* is on the Sunday menu at the *Black Cat* in Shar'a Sana'a.

Even less expensive is the *Al-Mansur* restaurant (Shar'a 24 December 33) whose *shish kebab* is recommended, while for those mid-afternoon Italian pastries, there's the small café in Shar'a 24 December run by FIDAT. 'Watching the world go by' is best done from one of the garden bars along the corniche or at the Caffé Aurora in Cathedral Square.

Pasta is eaten not only by the Italian community, but also very widely by Libyans, who also enjoy olives, white cheese with bread, tunny sandwiches, soup and rice.

There are few authentic Libyan dishes left, apart from *kuskus*, a meat stew served with polenta called *bazin*, and the *zumita*, a spiced dish of roasted barley.

During the Islamic month of Ramadan a typical breakfast (the first meal of the night, taken after sunset) could consist of *sharba*, which is a peppery meat soup, olives, *halwa*, dates, milk, *kuskus*, salad, radishes, rice with sauce and fried potatoes. Other special dishes might include *dulma* – minced lamb and rice in vine leaves; *muhallabia* – rice-pudding Libyan fashion; or *bakaiwa* – pastry stuffed with almonds and coated with honey.

Food does not concern a Tripolitan as much as drink. Denied alcohol by the rule of Islam, he lingers over his tea or coffee, thick with sugar, as though reluctant to swallow the last drop.

15
Music and Dance

It may be something to do with the New Leisure, but certainly the arts in Libya have never flourished as they do today.

The poetry of Ali Fezzani, the plays of Sa'id Sarraj, the stories of Kamal Maqhur, the films of Fu'ad al-Ka'bazi, the photographs of Abdelmun'im Naji, the sculpture of Ali Qana, the paintings of Tahir al-Mughrabi and Ali Abani: these are merely the first representative names that spring to mind, and most of them are connected with several disciplines: al-Laqwiri writes stories and plays, Ali Qana also paints, al-Ka'bazi is an artist and poet.

But the art of Libya *par excellence* is music, both instrumental and vocal.

If you switch the radio on in Tripoli, you will hear hours of music every day, except during Ramadan, when the time allotted to entertainment is reduced. Popular Libyan songs concern disappointed love, haughty women, anguish at parting, and nostalgia. Improvisation is still characteristic of the best Libyan music (solos must begin and end in the same key), and sadness, *saudade*, still inseparable from the pathetic quarter-tone that bewitched the Andalusian ear to such an extent that 'Spanish' music to the untutored really signifies 'Arab' music.

One of the young singers popular in Tripoli at the moment is Khalid Sa'id: these are the words of his record *Tawali*, written in Tripolitanian colloquial by Mas'ud al-Qiblawi and set to music by 'Ali Mahir.

The nearest equivalent to this style in the West is the blues. My very free version is intended to approximate to the tone rather than to convey literal accuracy.

Tawali, murawwah tawali *li-sighari wa li-watani 'l-ghali,* *li-nasi wa 'ishrat jirani,* *li-bui wa ummi wa 'ayali.*	*I wanna go home, straight back,* *to my kids and my shack,* *to my folks and the guys next door,* *to Momma and Pop and the girl next* *door.*
Tawali raj'a li-hibabi, *yakfi min al-ghurba, ya ashabi,*	*I wanna go back to where I started,* *I'm sick to death of being broken-* *hearted,*
wa 'l-bu'd illi mughayyir hali.	*I got the terrible homesick blues.*

Among the instruments used in Libya are *al-'ud* (the original lute), a drum called the *darbuka*, the sitar, a relative of the bagpipe called the *zukra,*a two-horned variety of flute called the *maqruna,* a type of violin called the *rabad,* a five-octave flute: the *nai,* and various tambourines with or without metal discs – *bindir, duft,* and *tar.*

A Libyan folklore group organised by the Government in 1963 has had great success in festivals at Sabratha, Tripoli, and abroad, probably because it combines very skilfully indigenous African dance rhythms with international Arab music. Most dances are of Tuareg inspiration. Bells and hand-clapping establish a rhythm which is then maintained at length, gradually reaching a climax, and suddenly dying away. The dance of girls balancing water-jugs on their heads, the dance of the old man invigorated by music of his youth, the gazelle solo, the lancers' quadrille: all are products of the vast spaces and long nights of the south, and owe little to neighbouring Arab countries, and least of all to Europe. The perennial authentic spirit of Libya hovers over the orchestra and dancers, resounding in every note.

16
Gargaresh and Tajura

Catacombs
If you make an appointment with the Controller of Antiquities of
the Western Provinces, whose offices are in Tripoli Castle, at ten
o'clock one morning as-Said Belgassem (the Tripolitanian form of the
name Abu 'l-Qasim) will accompany you in your car or taxi to the
recent excavations at Gargaresh, west of Giorgimpopoli.

Having turned left on to the first paved road after the 'Gargaresh'
signpost on the road to Zawia, you will bear right on to a sandy track
bearing the sign 'Excavations of Gargaresh'. After some five hundred
metres you will come to the temporary staff buildings of some of the
most exciting excavations yet undertaken in Libya. The site was
discovered in May 1965 during work on a water-well being dug for
new houses. At a depth of seven metres the labourers struck a gallery
with frescoes of the Roman period. When the archaeologists arrived,
they soon discovered that the gallery extended in several directions to
form catacombs.

One extraordinary feature of the Gargaresh site is its immense area:
already some 15,000 square metres have been laboriously cleared, but
the true extent of the catacombs may surpass this provisional estimate
by far. The most interesting find so far is the frescoed tomb or temple
discovered first. Fragments of Latin inscriptions, unidentifiable Roman
bronze coins, a marble capital, and various amphorae and crude
terra-cotta sherds have come to light. A fresco, on plaster, once brightly
coloured but now faded and partly disintegrated, appears to represent
a serpent entwined round a (palm?) tree between Adam and Eve.

Another shows a person on a donkey, and may represent Christ
entering Jerusalem on Palm Sunday. A third, to the left of Eve, can be

identified as the lower body of a priest in his robes, while a similar, complete, fresco with a torch in the priest's right hand, can be seen opposite the first.

Tomb of Aelia Arisuth

The recently-discovered catacombs may be Christian, but there can be little doubt that the tomb of Aelia Arisuth (further west) is Mithraic in origin, judging from the inscription found by Weber on first entering the subterranean chamber: *quae lea jacet*, 'lion' having been one of the stages of Mithraic initiation. The noble portrait of Aelia dates to the fourth century A.D. Much of its lustre has vanished in the course of centuries, but it clearly belongs to the brilliant school of al-Fayyum, whose other works grace the Egyptian Museum in Cairo and London's British Museum. Below the tomb another artist has depicted an exciting chariot-race, presumably to symbolise the course of life. The two termini are carefully painted, while the charioteers' tumbling and swerving uncannily seem to enliven the silent tomb with gaiety and noise.

The tomb may also have been a refuge of fourth-century devotees of Mithras, the Indo-European god of light and truth whose cult, introduced to Rome in 70 B.C., became the greatest threat to Christianity in its final struggle with ancient paganism. The Trinity concept and the birthday of Mithras (December 25th) were both incorporated into Christianity but, despite official patronage (one Antonine even built a Mithraic shrine), the cult of the Persian deity lost ground in competition with Jesus Christ. The Comforter, sacrificing the bull to ensure rebirth and renewal, gave way to the Saviour, a suffering human being with whom the masses could readily identify. Let no one think, however, that the Mediator and heliolatry ever died. Centuries earlier Plato could adore the Sun as the highest material symbol of Infinite Good; centuries later *le Roi Soleil* emulated the Roman union of absolutism in the State with religious authority.

Tajura

It seems that at last we have discovered *Turris ad Algam* ('the tower

by seaweed') recorded as being near the modern Tajura, an oasis
seventeen kilometres east of Tripoli, past the characteristic camel-
market of Suq al-Jum'a. *Turris ad Algam*, eleven kilometres east of
Tajura, appears to have been a fashionable seaside resort for wealthy
citizens of Oea. It was already inhabited by the middle of the second
century and appears to have been abandoned by the end of the fifth
century, possibly as a result of warfare. The modern visitor to these
ancient villas and baths may admire three hundred square metres of
mosaic floors, and incomplete columns, but it is quite clear that the
site already excavated is only partial: while strolling back along the
shore in the direction of Tajura I noticed two patches of mosaic
fragments embedded in the ground.

A drive round fertile Tajura must include a visit to the Great Mosque
of Murad Agha, with its classical columns from Leptis Magna. The
mosque is in the central square of the quiet town, and may be visited
at all times except on Fridays and at hours of prayer.

17
Giorgimpopoli

A fairy story.

Once upon a time – say 1912 – there was a lay priest called Giorgini who was given land outside Tripoli between a former Turkish military post at kilometre 1 on the Zawia road and the next Turkish post at kilometre 3.5. A florist called Finocchiaro was given land between Giorgini's and kilometre 5 – the beginning of the settlement of Qarqarash, (or Gargaresh) originally Qaraqush, the name of a Turkish buccaneer who built a castle in 1194 in the area that now bears his name. He was killed at Waddan in 609 A.H. (1212-13 A.D.). Both Giorgini's concession and that of Finocchiaro extended from the sea to the Gurgi road.

Every Tripoli resident knows the rest: Giorgimpopoli and Floropoli (as the two holdings soon became known) were gradually sold off, and though descendants of Giorgini and Finocchiaro still live in Tripoli, the ownership of this fabulously valuable area has passed to Libyan landlords, who have devised impressive construction schemes, and developed the district beyond the Italians' wildest dreams.

Giorgimpopoli runs from the Wadi Majnin to the present Bowlarena Club, and Floropoli continues westward as far as the beginning of Gargaresh.

At Wheelus Air Base – at the opposite end of Tripoli – the American community is sealed off hermetically, as in a polythene bag. Giorgimpopoli and Floropoli give the impression of aspiring to the condition of Wheelus, but infusions of Libyan and European families dotted at intervals in the solid blocks of American-rented villas do help to dispel the atmosphere of Little California. Tripoli is, of course, on the

TRIPOLI

same latitude as Atlanta, Tucson, or Los Angeles: Texas and Californians find the climate similar and conditions in some ways comparable.

Tenpin bowling, American matrons in Bermuda shorts, hot dogs at the Chicken on Wheels, an Oil Companies' School: nothing is lacking to make homesick Oklahomans feel at home. But because home has to be best, U.S. residents of Giorgimpopoli like to complain: about the drainage, the rents, the sand-tracks which make driving up to your house from the coast road seem like an adventure along the Grand Canyon, the cost of food, the imagined scarcity of consumer goods, the difficulties with cooks and houseboys. . . .

The list is endless. And yet they stay. Some Americans came to Tripoli during World War II and preferred to avoid repatriation when it was over. Some are moved by a real desire to pool their special talents with the resources of Libya's small but vital professional-technical élite. Whether simply attracted by high salaries and challenging assignments in the desert, or – perhaps in some cases – by the excitement of living in Libya, most of them stay beyond their initial contract.

Giorgimpopoli has its own banks, travel agents and supermarket. The shop signs* give the impression of being knocked up hastily for a Disney comedy: *Sheriff Shop, Floropoli Butcher, Sahara Butcher, Extra Butcher, S. Ventre Sales & Service of Sanitary Items, Uncle Sam Stores, Muktar Bookshop, Toytown School Lunch, Carmen Beauty Salon, Riviera Shop, Dabnun Dime Store*, and the dazzling *New Marketing Animals and Poultry Feed.* Just next to *Fresh Eggs & Vegetable* is *The House of Glamour Perfumery Mary Quant.* There is a *Blue Shop* and a *Green Shop: Tavola Calda* competes with the *Guy and Joe Snack Bar.* For sheer grotesque fantasy, however, I commend *Hot Meals: Red Cat.* I've never eaten there.

* *Signs in languages other than Arabic were taken down in September 1969 by order of the Revolutionary Command Council.*

64

11 Jam'a Gurgi: Patio.

12 Jam'a Gurgi:
    Interior.

13   Old City: Covered Textile Market.

14 S. Maria degli Angeli: the High Altar, with Mancinelli's painting.

15 Tripoli Castle: Ramparts, showing the Cathedral Dome.

16 New Tripoli: Aerial view, with the octagonal Galleria De Bono in the centre.

17   Roman Catholic Cathedral.

18   Gardens at Gazelle Jetty, showing part of an olive press found near al-Qusbat.

19   Villa Volpi: Courtyard with stone parterre.

18
Tripoli Now

In 1900 the population of Tripoli was 25,000: precisely that esti-
mated for 1790. But the present century has seen the city's population
virtually double every twenty years: from 50,000 in 1920 to 100,000
in 1940, and 200,000 in 1960.

The boundaries will extend even further, continuing southward
along the Swani road, west beyond Gargaresh, and east to Mellaha.
There is so much land available in these directions that it would be a
pity to build more in the centre of Tripoli, thereby destroying buildings of historical interest and architectural beauty.

One such is the vast, airy Galleria de Bono, with the Romagna
restaurant, open-arched on all four sides. Another is the neo-Romanes-
que Cathedral, begun in 1923 and completed in 1928, when it replaced
S. Maria degli Angeli as the Cathedral of Tripoli. A third is the former
Palace, with its gracious loggias and gilded domes, glistening white
by day and illuminated on all festive evenings, including every
Thursday.

Behind the former Palace is the middle-class residential suburb of
Garden City, radiating in all directions from Golden Medal Square,
known also as Garden City Circle. Most of the foreign embassies and
legations are to be found in this area, whose main artery is Shar'a Ben
Ashur.

Shopping for food is done at little local shops, but supermarkets
exist for those who want to do all their weekly shopping at once.

Education
Everywhere one sees the black uniform of school children running
to and from school. Such is the demand for education in modern

Libya that a shift system has to be operated in order to cope with the rush.

Just as there are two legal systems in Libya: the religious system based on the Qur'an, and the secular system based on the Napoleonic code by way of Egyptian adaptations, so there are two university structures: the Islamic University of as-Said Muhammad bin Ali as-Sanusi (with headquarters at al-Baida, in Cyrenaica) and the secular University of Libya. The secular University is divided into faculties for the Arts and Education, Law, and Commerce and Economics – all in Benghazi, and Science, Teacher-Training, and Technology – just outside Tripoli at the rural district of Sidi al-Misri. The humanities are taught in Arabic, and the sciences in English.

Education, like so much else in new Tripoli, is a lesson in partnership between the national element and foreign experts hired to ensure that the best guidance and facilities are available to the most important generation of all – the next one.

Wealth from Oil

The importance of the oil industry in arid countries where farmers fight a losing battle against a hostile climate is accentuated in Libya. Before Libya became independent in 1951, the great majority of the population of a million and a quarter were largely illiterate, depending for subsistence on sufficient rainfall. Exports were so small that without massive contributions of aid from Britain and the United States the people would have starved.

Within two decades, however, the international oil industry has brought unimagined wealth to Libya: from being one of the poorest nations in the world, she has become one of the richest, thanks to aggressive exploration for oil on the part of the companies, who rent concessions, and the far-sighted planning of the Government, who own the land. For the Government is well aware of the danger of relying too heavily on oil revenues, and is building up Libya's agriculture by financial subsidy and technical guidance. Fishing, forestry, and tourism all require urgent development, but there is no doubt that Tripoli's tremendous growth will soon be paralleled elsewhere in the country.

Though no more than ten thousand Libyans are directly employed by oil companies, their salaries benefit a much larger number. A lorry-mechanic servicing company vehicles may earn a hundred pounds a month, whereas before the arrival of the companies there would have been no job for him; if one had been found it would have paid much less. Contractors to oil companies flourish in proportion: merchants, caterers, transportation firms, construction consortiums; in particular, landowners. Only Libyan nationals may own property in the Kingdom, and demand is likely to outrun the availability of houses for many years because of the rapidly increasing population, and the constantly rising standard of living that demands better houses. The demand from oil companies for accommodation for their staff is especially keen.

In 1961 there were twenty-seven oil companies operating in Libya, holding between them a total of eighty-seven concession deeds; in 1967, forty-two companies held a hundred and thirty-six concessions. Libya dispatched twenty-five shipments totalling 5,248,104 barrels in 1961; in 1966 oil ports loaded 1,566 shipments accounting for 547,250,643 barrels. This rate of increase shows no sign of slackening, as Occidental Oil Co. of Libya have recently struck huge reserves in the Syrtic Desert, and have begun to export oil from their Zuwaitina terminal.

According to the Economic Development Law of 1963, 70% of revenues from oil exports were assigned to a development fund. The first Five-Year Development Plan was concluded in 1967, and a second plan immediately put into effect.

Hassi Atshan, in west Fezzan, was the scene of the first post-war oil strike, but by far the greater proportion of finds have been made in the Syrtic Desert, in concentric circles round Oasis Oil's Dahra field and Esso Standard's Zelten. Companies fly out their own aircraft to strips near their camps. The national air line even calls at the oil terminal of Marsa Brega on some flights between Tripoli and Benghazi.

Conditions in these oil camps bear little resemblance to rough conditions twenty years ago. Now two men share an air-conditioned trailer in great comfort, with showers. The catering is contracted out to a firm which *has* to supply the best in order to keep the contract.

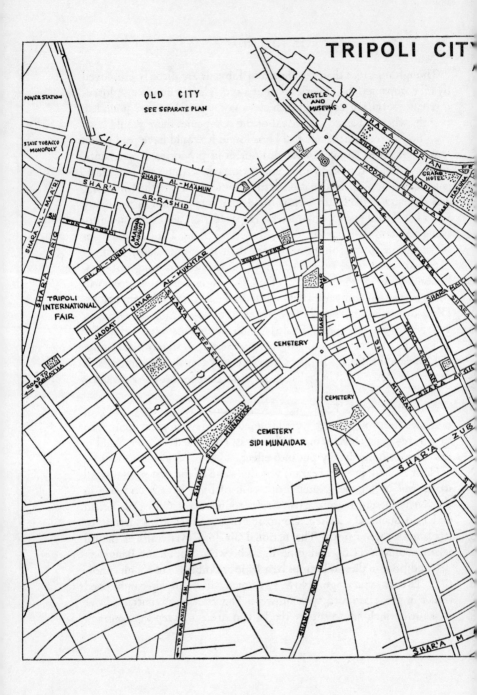

TRIPOLI CITY

POWER STATION

OLD CITY
SEE SEPARATE PLAN

CASTLE AND MUSEUMS

STATE TOBACCO MONOPOLY

SHAR'A AL-MA'AMUN

SHAR'A AR-RASHID

SHAR'A AL-MAARI

SH

SHAR'A TARIQ

TRIQ AR-RUH

MAIDAN 9 AUGUST

EL AL-KINDI

UMAR

JADDAT

SHAR'A AL-MUKHTAR

SHAR'A RAFFAELLO

SHAR'A SEKKA

CEMETERY

SHAR'A QMR

IBN AL

SHAR'A MIZRAN

SHAR'A ADRIAN

SHAR'A AL-BADDA

GRAND HOTEL

JADDAT

SFIGLIA

MASJIDA

SHAR'A PEFFEBERI

TRIPOLI INTERNATIONAL FAIR

SHAR'A HATI

SHAR'A SHAR'A

SHAR'A KUSTANTINA

SHAR'A AFRIS

ROAD TO SABRATHA

CEMETERY

MIZRAN

SHAR'A ZUG

CEMETERY SIDI MUNAIDAR

SHAR'A SIDI MUNAIDAR

SHAR'A SRIM

SH AS

TO BAB ACCRA

SHAR'A ABU HARIDA

SHAR'A M

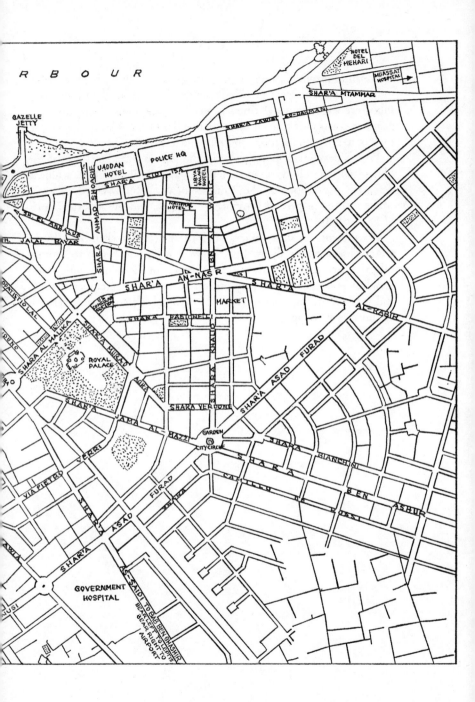

Companies provide a rest-room with games facilities, tape-recorder, radio, and perhaps even a golf course, tennis court or swimming pool. Films are shown several times a week. At least one company runs training centres for Libyan personnel, and a Desert Library Service to each of its Saharan locations and pipeline terminal.

Tripoli developed sporadically in the past as a trading post of the Phoenicians, a colony of ancient Rome and mediaeval Byzantium, a defensive stronghold of the Knights of St. John manned to assist Malta in time of peril, a province of Turkey, and the 'Fourth Shore' of Fascist Italy.

The present city shows traces of all these periods, when the Libyans were subservient to aliens. But the face of Tripoli began to acquire Libyan characteristics with the revolution for 'freedom, unity, and socialism' carried out by army officers at dawn on September 1, 1969, and it is true to say that in terms of national self-confidence, Tripoli has now come of age.

Further Reading

The best book on Tripoli's history takes the tale up only to the collapse of Turkish rule: it is the late Ettore Rossi's scholarly *Storia di Tripoli e della Tripolitania dalla conquista araba al* 1911 (Rome: Istituto per l'Oriente, 1968). Fortunately John Wright's volume on *Libya* in the 'Nations of the modern world' series (London: Benn, 1969) brings the story right up to date.

To keep abreast of archaeological discoveries in Tripoli and its surroundings, subscribe to the indispensable *Libya Antiqua* (Tripoli: Department of Antiquities, annually). A. di Vita studied the Tajura villa complex in the *Archaeological News* and supplement to Vol. II (1965), while the Gargaresh catacombs were first reported by Taha Bakir in Vol. III-IV (1966-67).

Of the many accounts of Tripoli City scattered throughout more general books in English I recommend those in H. S. Cowper's *Hill of the Graces* (Methuen, 1897), C. W. Furlong's *Gateway to the Sahara* (Chapman and Hall, 1909), Angelo Piccioli's *Magic gate of the Sahara* (Methuen, 1935), Knud Holmboe's *Desert encounter* (Harrap, 1936), and Mary Berenson's *Vicarious trip to the Barbary Coast* (Constable, 1938).

Two notable women's books have been written about Tripoli. Miss Tully's *Letters written during a ten years' residence at the Court of Tripoli* (1816) has been reprinted with a valuable introduction by Seton Dearden (London: Barker, 1957). Agnes Newton Keith's nine years in Libya were described in her *Children of Allah* (London: Michael Joseph, 1966). The Emma Laing story is told at greater length in *Missions to the Niger* (Vol. 1), edited by E. W. Bovill and published for the Hakluyt Society by the Cambridge University Press in 1964.

Little has been published recently on Tripoli's social customs, but Muhammad Abdelkafi's excellent *Weddings in Tripolitania* (Tripoli: Ministry of Information, 1966) devotes fifteen pages to marriage customs in the city. The Tripoli dialect can be learnt from C. P. Bradburne's two-volume *Basic Tripolitanian Arabic* (New York: Mobil Oil, 1962).

Index and Pronunciation Guide

Stressed syllables are accented. Numbers in italics refer to the illustrations

73